POWWOWS, FAT CATS,

AND OTHER

INDIAN TALES

BY

E. DONALD TWO-RIVERS

Mammoth Publications
Lawrence, Kansas 66044

ISBN 978-0-9800102-6-8
2nd printing 2009

Cover Design by Randi Robin
Cover Art by Chris Pappan
Production coordinated by Nora Lloyd
Book Design by Denise Low
Printing by Lightning Source

The author wishes to thank those who helped get this
collection together: Beverly Moeser, Nora Lloyd, Chris Pappan,
Randi Robin, Denise Low, and Richard Ginsburg.

Mammoth Publications
1916 Stratford Rd. Lawrence, Kansas 66044

mammothpubs@hotmail.com

www.mammothpublications.com

TABLE OF CONTENTS

OLD DOG SOLDIER

I'll not speak
   in vision talk tongue
   with eyes cast to the ground.

I'll not sing chants nor burn sage
   to ease troubled minds.
I'll not greet you with Hollywood's
 TV Indian "love-you-whitey" salutations.

What you'll hear might make you squirm.

Don't sit there and see me
   as buckskin token
   because I'm a dog soldier,
a dog soldier schooled on city streets,
   an urban Indian cast aside
   by the swagger of technology.
Don't expect concepts
   that will assign artifact status
   to the history of my people.

Manifest Destiny still haunts
 our collective minds.

KA-WE-GOON-A-BEK

For Nancy Johnson, my mom, inspired by
Andrew Johnson, my cousin

Could this nation know your spirit,
presidents would salute and bow.
Ka-We-Goon-A-Bek, I remember watching
your hands at task.
They flew across the scrub board,
efficient hands that molded survival
and fed us values to live by.
You leaned into your work,
hair cascading over shoulders like a dancer's
shawl.
Sunlight silhouetted your body
and I thought you the most beautiful of women.
Miigwech, Ka-We-Goon-A-Bek, for your work
ethic.

Singing softly, etching me an Indian song for
those hard times,
Miigwech, Ka-We-Goon-A-Bek,
for the tenacity to survive
demanding situations with a smile and a joke.

Your sojourner's heart showed how to cast aside
the yoke of ethnic identity
and to peer into the world's similarities,
that tolerance of others leads to an inner peace.
Those humble moments that you handed me taught
me the meaning of that beauty surrounding me.
Wherever my path carries me in this journey,
my eyes seek that beauty

and drink it up like a cup of cold spring water on
a hot July afternoon.
Miigwech, Ka-We-Goon-A-Bek, for that gift.

Those first grains of wild rice you fed me
nourished my body and created
a foundation of confidence.
You whispered,
"To leap is to live."
Could this nation know your spirit,
presidents would salute and bow.
Miigwech, Ka-We-Goon-A-Bek,
Miigwech, Anishinaabe-kwe

AS A CHILD
   Dedicated to my elders

As a child:
I heard those stories that define *Anishinaanbeg*—
love's quiet tales, war legends,
Windigo's mystery, Loon's magic.
From my elders: lessons of joy and life,
of trap lines and respect,
how to walk with reverence in the bush,
to paddle a canoe.

I remember so clearly those soft brown faces,
sparkling eyes and sharp tongues.
Like shafts of morning sunlight,
they urge you forward
with the caress of confidence.
Islands of stability, they share wisdom
with gazes that warm the coldest soul.

They stand proud, the old ones,
poised to give knowledge
to soften life's sharp sting.

They teach wisdom's vision
carved from years of experience.
Spiritual keepers of sacred insights,
they give hope, knowledge and a gentle touch.
In dark eyes you see wisdom.
It's a tightly fashioned vision.

Bow in respect. Touch a weathered hand.
Holding those feathers, praying gentle prayers,
they fashion our future with calculated steps.
They pray for our world's wellness.
Honor them always, the elders of all nations.

RECLUSE

The world was feverish with snow!
I was nine years old and a curious
Indian child living in a mystical place,
a strong magical place, rich with Indian history.
It was a granite kingdom
ruled by the heartbeat of Mother Earth
and guarded by Jack Pines
that pierced the horizon across a frozen lake.

A recluse hermit of my childhood years,
a feared philosopher children whispered about,
pulled his toboggan, panting and squinting.

A smile melts your frown.
Wrapping a red scarf around your ancient throat,
you said I was dammed by a lack of innocence.
You trailed your shadow behind you,
intent on the sole purpose of survival.

Forty years later I remember clearly
the crunch of work boots on frozen snow,
the smell of your pipe.
I can recall your cynical laugh
spouting philosophy I somehow understood.
I can remember your old body leaning
when you pulled your toboggan.
Your words echo clearly in my mind.

INDIAN LAND DANCING

Rice picking time:
canoes, adventure, brown-faced cousins.
Laughter pierces afternoon heat.
Boys at play; men at labor.
Venison treats and bannock too.

Events spiral to memories,
linking lives to time and history.
Culprit children frenzied with imagination:
Sticks stir small hands to mock battle,
moments of concentrated joy,
lessons in a green galaxy
of ferns and cedars and pine trees.

Drums caress the night air,
voices sing over hills and valleys.
Ceremonial jingle dresses, flutter of shawls.
The fancy dancer twirls, dips to earth, and flies.
He dances east, west, south, and north
paying respectful homage with a lively step.

It was rice picking time:
I thought all of Indian land danced.
Brown-faced women smile, dance,
hands on curvy hips, black braids bouncing.
Their reflections dance on water's top.
A young boy, I thought
all of Indian land was dancing.

OLD MAN AND RENEGADE BOY

Storyteller pulls me into his life experiences.
Legends' shadows reflect in the playful twinkle
of his smiling eye.
Oh, how I loved this man patting my head,
showing me how to split wood.
The moment is mine: his storyteller's gift.

Old man teaches, showing me the scars
of blazing marks that bring life
to the remnants of the Dawson Trail story.
Renegade boy, bastard of *Anishinaabe* nights,
shows scars of his own story,
spoken in tears that spill from rims of his eyes.

I bend over an old bird's nest,
brittle kindling, licked into flames.
An eddy's wooden match hisses
and tea warms my belly.
Telling stories adds dimension
to the winter camp.
Lighting his pipe he smiled and said,
"This is the life!"
The moment is mine: storyteller's gift.

He made me proud of everything I was.
He gave me that, then went away.
I was pushed into torrid sun, armed with lessons
taught with love over tea and bannock
and the smell of his pipe.
Always dad, but never father,
he must have power.
His memory returns to visit now and then
when decisions are to be made.
The moment is mine: storyteller's gift.

BOXING LESSONS

A craftsman's skilled hands
stroke fine wood with loving touch
then punches me playfully, shows me moves.
Bob, weave, jab and counter.

Happy afternoons in August sun,
then horrible moments, crashing dreams,
my brown face burning with shame.
I hold trembling hands tightly over ears
screaming silently in dread. I recall
bitter words uttered in whiskeyed anger.

"That bastard son of yours."
In stoic Indian silence she'd take
the brunt of verbal assault.
Bob, weave, jab and counter.

Nightmares in August's darkness
bob, weave, jab and counter.
Sweat and tears falling,
crying and exhausted on mother earth's breast,
trembling quietly, cursing both for being human.
I never forgive myself for what I didn't know.

Suicidal I stared at images in a pond,
a confusing array of wavelets.
Throat stinging, burning and etching
nightmare of shame on my soul.
Willows and pine branches slapping
my face but not ending that shame.
Running hard, each step echo's loudly
"Bastard." "Bastard."
Bastard running, hating furiously
pain that raked every fiber.

Heart burning, bursting with regret,
running, running, running Bastard
past beaver dam, blue berry patch, poplar trees
through marsh into pine grove
with a Canadian jay squawking overhead.
Each step trying to run away from the hurt
the pain, the words, from myself
"Bastard running, running Bastard."
Bob, weave, jab and counter.

SCOUTS SCOUTING

In *Sapawe*
beneath birch, pine and cedar;
atop a high granite hill
protruding from amongst
other windswept granite hills,
life unfolded.
Nature revealed little lessons,
including tourists.

You explorers,
with technologically advanced
paddles and cameras and soaring spirits,
look around you
with an appreciative eye,
never see us nor feel our presence.

Camping at lake's end
at day's end
singing praises around campfire—
did you know we were there?

We lay atop a cliff,
a granite cliff on the soft cool moss
where the winds carried your smell
and we watched you.

TIME OF THE *WINDIGO*

Beast-symbol of madness and hunger—
northern terror. Fear is real.
They are Ice Giants with frozen evil hearts.
In wigwams, old ones finger medicine bundles.
Strange happenings, moving kettles:
Windigo stalks the winter night.
Ma'iingan howls into chilled stillness
Waaboozoog huddle in fear under a cedar tree.
The m*ooz* was still, deer pawed frozen soil.
An owl peers into the darkness.
A chickadee sits silent in the breeze.

Reddened sky, missing trails,
sage and cedar burning—
children sigh and cry.
Old ones listen to the silence,
whisper in quiet tones,
and warm sticks of sumac.

Fingering medicine bundles,
they utter quiet prayers.
Babies in *dikinaaganan* are faced sacred directions.
The *Windigo* warrior weasel chews the heart.
The wigwams shake, lightning bolts pierce
Ice Giant's evil heart to end the madness.

The fear is real.
In wigwams of *Anishinaabe*, children cry.
Old ones finger medicine bundles praying.
It is the time of the *Windigo*.

MOM'S POEM:
ANOTHER MUSKIE LANDED

"Don't you ever be afraid to do what's right!"

Mother gave to me the stuff for hard battles,
indignant eyes to peer through haze,
to spot weakness in those who would deny me.
Fighting a muskie until it was a gasping mass
of fins, scales and eyes blinking confused,
she approached life's hard times with a smile.

She'd cut deals with big city buyers
wanting her hand-crafted buckskin coats
for nothing more than a promise.
Sweat glistened on her Indian forehead
pulling fish nets through iced waters.

I admired her tenacity and comforted her
in those quiet, lonely moments.
Neither rains nor driving snows
could make her shake in fear.
As a child I watched her gentle hands
forge out a meal from practically nothing
with skill and confidence.
With her man she worked side by side
then cooked a meal fit for a king.
When the fool left us I knew he'd lost.
She smiled her confidence.
It shone beautiful on her lovely face
and I understood another muskie was landed.

MA'IIN-GAN
Wolf's Spirit

Tail and ears held high,
you rule the empire we shared
in childhood years of races with wind.
Your image stilled my heart.
Your spirit's served me well, *Ma'iin-gan.*
My head is held high just as I saw,
tail of leadership held high
by he who was your father.
Proud and strong you are, a hunter of skill.
sharing a hunting ground
with my own father, also a hunter of skill.

So many moons have passed.
Changes, so many changes.
In a big city where wolves and Indians
are imprisoned in a zoo
I recall your winter's night prayer
and I walk with head held high and sure step
on concrete city streets where I see
need of spiritual cleansing,
where sweat lodge calls to deadened ears
of brother warriors crawling on bleeding knees
in early morning grime of Wilson Avenue.
My heart cries *Ma'iin-gan,*
for sisters who hear not the urgent whispers,
prostituting themselves
for distilled poison and the burn of cocaine
in nostrils no longer knowing
sweetness of pine, cedar or sage.
Ma'iin-gan, Ma'iin-gan
Ma'iin-gan, Ma'iin-gan.

ODE TO A RIVER

Sitting on a river's edge.
watching sun rays dance
small wavelet to small wavelet.
Wah-shi-kii-shi-kuk
the Indian's call it.
Shade tree comforting me.
Gentle wind exciting the air
to caress my brown face.
My breath is captured
by this river's humble majesty.

This spot where I repose
feels like a place
where spirits would dance and feast.
Where time has preserved
a sense of mystery,
where harsh emotions
are released on quiet days.
Old campfire, deer trails to water's edge
confirm my thoughts.
This is a place where a small Indian boy
can sit dreaming big dreams.

OJIBWA FISHERMAN

The pink of a new day colors his thoughts.
Calloused hands pull nets,
hands hardened and stiff from labor.
His laugh echoes from generations
of respect for mother earth and life.
A woodpecker hammers for food,
a king-fisher sails low on the water's surface.
Cold water slaps the canoe hull,
the wind sings a gentle lullaby.

A native heart, tender and loving,
dark fluid eyes radiate a smile,
whispering soft melodic words,
that float like water-lily flowers.
A spider scurries across its world
and overhead a hawk searches for prey.

He speaks freedom words
on *Sapawe* Lake, that fisherman.
He speaks sounds not altered by time,
words more felt than understood.
Silhouetted against the dark morning sky,
the pink of a new day colors my thoughts.

PASSING THROUGH

I'm not some artifact!
Look, I'm sitting here before you naked.
So why do you look at me
like you're looking at the past?
I'm the one you pinched on the ass
in the elevator.
I'm not a relic dancing out of a history book
to sit on State Street watching.

I've never been what anyone wanted,
never a part of any colonial road show

except one time I met this woman
in a Chicago bar
who wanted me to paint my face,
tie her to her bed
and take her with a warrior's
ardent yell.
I didn't understand "ardent,"
so I jumped her bones.

In my most truthful moments
I'll admit I got into it until neighbors
threatened to call the cops.
At that point I helped myself
to the money in her purse
and left her tied to the bed cursing.
But what the hell?
She told me I could have what I needed.
I was homeless, for Christ's sake.
So don't look at me
like I was some artifact.

L.A. LADY IN RED
for Lola Paint of LA

Hollywood redskins in blue-top Ford.
Hollywood night with a new friend, LA lady
in a red dress—
so this was where you rock and rolled?
Shrimp Boat of late night parties,
singing 49's with skins from everywhere,
fake diamonds made us laugh.
I hugged up to sweet LA lady in red.

Laughing at me for being a Cubs fan
"So how many times you vote, Chicago man?"
teasing and laughing about Chicago politics,
called me Midwest gangster
in blue jean cut-offs.
My mood molded to the softness of her body.
Her kisses fired passion in the night,
LA lady in red treating me like a movie star.

Morning sun climbing over mountains
kept me looking east.
following shadows, watching the sun setting—
Pacific coast and my eyes looking East.
My heart followed my eyes.
A few weeks we laughed and loved.
Good-bye, farewell, pretty LA lady in red.

SAD SONGS
Another scene from *Squeaky Moccasins*

A little boy with big eyes,
messed hair, pouting lips
sits ashamed and afraid with no hope,
sits Indian-style on the floor listening
to despondent words of a hillbilly song.

She's washing dishes and crying blues.
Oh, how she laments looking at her boy
in ragged gym shoes sitting
like an Indian on an Indian rug
on the hard floor of the living room.

How different life might have been
if she hadn't gotten pregnant.
She might have married a prince.
"I still have good looks."

"The kid," she thinks, "has got to go..."
and he does.

ROAD CREW

Feeling macho in Kodiak boots, no shirt,
hungered looks of suburban women
in passing cars make me feel good.

I dream of Sugar Spoon,
a sweet taste of sin in younger summers.
She whispered lewd promises.
In summer rains she kept them.

>Brown flames of desire
>reflect hot in Ojibwa eyes.
>sweat pouring, stinging and lustful,
>She whispers my name.
>I kiss sweat that ran
>in small rivulets between her thighs.
>Her skin, brown and clean and sweet
>in Canada's afternoon sun
>sears shyness from exploring fingers.
>She whispers my name.
>she guides me to where
>I've never been before,
>my innocence melting like morning
>mist before the sun's torrid glare.
>Breathing short gasps of desire,
>wanting the moment to last forever,
>I cannot get enough
>of her Indian passion.
>Lips, full and sensual and damp,
>kiss away all reason.
>She whispers my name.

The August sun attacks my strength
and I return to road crew toiling.

SHE SINGS AS SHE DANCES

A bare-breasted dancer,
a fallen angel, dancing topless
in a wooded forest of lust,
a goddess of Greek mythology
on windswept prairies of America.
She sways to an Indian rhythm
like billowing clouds embracing destiny.
Her soft voice flexes like
northern moss whispering promises.

Small brown hands caress small brown breasts,
delicate fingers dance across her nakedness.
She excites and hypnotizes.
Beauty and grace dance the night away
on the windswept prairies of America.
The singing dancer's words float on smoky air,
falling from fading rainbows.
Somewhere on windswept prairies of America
she dances.

A MOMENT TOO SOON

I fondle a Cheyenne girl,
thinking sinful thoughts,
chewing a twig in my best James Dean pose
and thinking about home.
She rubs my skinny legs
leans her head against my chest
then turns her face away.
I feel city in my soul
and tears roll down my cheek.

She didn't want my name.
To address each other we merely say,
"Hey you, with the hippie hair!
I grasped her beauty,
that Cheyenne girl,
clutched her with my eyes.
I lost my past those few days
walking Lincoln Park
with the long-legged girl
and always laughing.

But she boarded a Greyhound bus west
a moment before I fell in love.

BRIEF ENCOUNTERS

He hurries down Argyle Avenue
to a day's work counting blessings.
Pan-handlers eye him hopefully
and shuffle a few steps,
idled hands outstretched.
He's seen them huddled in doorways
in the early morning cold.

A young street-walking woman
glues her attention to a blue Chevy.
It slows then speeds away.
He watches her work the street,
body language tainted by desperation.
She steps aside for a moment
stands shivering in a deserted doorway.
Her mouth is dry and hurting.
Crack pipes leave her agitated and scared.

She hums a tune to add yet another
layer of justification to her bruised facade.
As she struts her stuff on Broadway,
tricks and wind plummet to a numbing chill.
Her passion's been assassinated by cold dollars
that strange men press into her young hands,
ransom for their perversions.

TO AN ACTRESS

You got something I want a lot of.
It's that northern-pine loving
Stones were hissing in the sweat lodge.
Steam blew in my eye and I heard
your sigh somewhere deep inside.

My emotions are floating like water lilies
in a pond or is it like the clouds
that straddle the atmosphere,
this feeling that starts
way down low in my belly
and wants to scream for joy and leap
after the rainbow on a summer day.
In the sweat lodge the stones are hissing.

I feel like a dancer dancing for understanding.
Twirling and dipping with feathers flying.
Hoping that with a new shadow will
come a new and better understanding.
You got something that I want a lot of.
It's that northern-pine-tree loving.
In the sweat lodge the stones are hissing.

WANNABE WARRIOR

Oh, the regrets
some people carry around
in their back pockets
like small boys tote stones,
throwing them
here and there
like temper tantrums.
You talk to people
like they were supposed to care.

You invent a past to compensate
for what you wanted but never could be.
Valor in battle?
A fairy tale you keep
up in your sleeve
like a switchblade knife,
a story tucked away
between shots
and cheap draught beer.

OLD NEIGHBOR

I talk to him every now and then
over in the old neighborhood.
He tells me that he hears voices
ever since the night we partied
under the El tracks by the graveyard.
He overdosed on Purple Barrel—LSD.

He tells me, "I hear them sometimes,
voices that plague me with visions
of violence and the stench of fear.
I stay hidden in my dad's place . . afraid.
I hear them crying, screaming, talking fast.
He turns away and looks up at the clouds.

"When that happens, my head burns hot,
eyes sting from sweat . . . stomach churns . . .
I can't look up . . .can't face anyone . . . .
I hear the voices singing mean songs
about everybody I ever knew.
Those same creatures in a comic book,
with teeth flashing, devour my flesh.

The voices penetrate night air,
driving me insane ever so slowly.
Why don't they shut up, leave me alone?"
He drifts to another place
and walks singing under the El tracks
by the graveyard in the old neighborhood.

DREAM SELLERS

Young revolutionaries willing to fight,
violent images crept into our art
and cold pistols warmed our pockets.
"Power to the people" we yelled,
Our trigger finger ached to caress
the head of Amerika then.
We raised angry fists
against the oppressor we were told about
by the gurus of our times with berets
at a cocky angle and an eye cast
to those coffers our idealism represented.

We put away revolutionary spirits
but still sometimes on quiet nights
the ghosts come dancing down the avenues
and the chants are remembered.
Sweat running down our arms now
is born from hard nights at labor.

Spokesmen of our revolution
are riding the crest to wealth.
They hardly look at us anymore unless
they want a vote or to sell us a gourmet meal.

SOUTHSIDE CITY SCENE

Used to be home to Illinois Truck Parts,
deserted now at Archer and Cermack,
a meadow of mud, motor oil, scrap iron,
concrete blocks and a galvanized storage shed
that leans into a February wind
like drunks on Clark Street shivering.
Only sturdy weeds grow in this meadow.

The Loop skyline does a waltz
of blinking lights
led by skeleton structures
of railroad capitalism that roared
a song of profits in ages past.

Silhouetted in predawn gloom,
a single seagull silently and gracefully
rides on gusts of winds.
He circles alone, solitary,
flight feathers spread.
The sight leaves me feeling
a melancholy sense of sorrow,
like that lone seagull
but I know that soon it will change.

BIG SHOULDERS SAGGING

Chicago's big shoulders are sagging
like some kind of surrealist sketch,
the Big Windy becoming disjointed figures
falling in a Chagall painting.
Ghosts of working men wander
aimlessly in valleys of depression.
Their numbers grow, becoming angered shards
within a hardened shell that protects.
Detroit's G.A. people are dying in the streets.

This is "Amerika," with a capital A!
Chicago's unemployed, "now permanent,"
walk in frightened circles
to join thousands more idled workers.
Children sing the national anthem,
pledge to be good but starving Americans.
Spell it with a capital A.

Amerika's work force is under attack,
big shoulders sagging.
Grab the cause, carry it like a torch.
The city that works cannot work now.
Its back is breaking now,
destiny controlled by callused hands.
Big shoulders sagging cannot, will not,
lead you where you need to go.

GLASS EYE COMMUNIQUÉ

My glass eye sees it all:

Jesus directed this while
Al Capone's biggest fan danced
in a gay bar nude.
Henry's best whore fell in love
with a gum-shoe cop.
He ran crying in Uptown winds,
sobbing and throwing punches
but hit only brick walls.

A bald-headed brother calling himself Leroy
followed Southern Belle into a nut house.
They let her go but kept him.
He tripped on LSD and started praying
to a cat named "Ears le Cat."
A foreign-speaking shrink qualified
his black ass to do the Thorazine Shuffle.
A year of group therapy and he quit shaking,
but he still chain smokes
and the brother spaces in mid sentence,
but he be all right, I hear.

Southern Belle got drunk and moved
to Rocky Top, Tennessee,
hooked up with a local clan-man named Bubba
and put on 115 pounds of radical racism
flavored by biscuits, gravy and grits.

My glass eye sees it all:
I told a girl in a north-side lounge
that I was Prince Charming
with a pearl-handled pistol in my pocket.
She smiled, licked her lips then grabbed my ass,

told me she was the Queen of Scriptures
and that she danced naked
with each eclipse of the sun.
That sounded like devil worship
to my urban Indian ass so I split the scene.

Wounded Knee happened but America
missed the whole point.
Boy Scouts sang dirty songs
about Barbara Bush and the price
of beer went up 11.5 percent.

A hair-lipped Korean refugee
called me a "something-or-another low-life."
I can't even begin to tell you
how that sounded—
but Walter Crinite called
the incident vulgar and racist
and Miss Winfrey suggested
that it might be newsworthy.

Landlords continued to exploit
their tenants of color
but let cockroaches and vermin
live rent free.
We banded together and tried
to run a Hispanic for alderman,
but it wasn't to be.
A sex-crazed madman stalked
the neighborhood boys with a promise
of learning a trade.
Their young mutilated bodies
were encased in concrete
and they never were paid.
And in between all of that
the Chicago Cubs had one

pretty good year.
An actor got elected president
and somehow our wild dreams started to fade.

I have seen it with my glass eye.
My glass eye sees it all.

GHOST DANCER'S STORY
for Walter, last poem of 1983

Visions of excitement flood his thoughts
riding the Greyhound south to Chi-town.
A mover in the fast lane,
this player dreams of "magazine-cover" women
in tight skirts and loose morals.
Sport cars, fancy threads, click of pool balls
and Saturday night emotions:
it is an elusive dream cloaked
in a pale-colored guise
that dissipates with his cash flow.

His became a dream fed by the
sensual tension of all-night card games,
harsh taste of beer and angry guitars.
He sought more:
sweet caress of reefer highs,
flaming blaze of LSD sunrises,
and finally the seductive sting
of the killing needle with its burn.
He could be seen nodding
in vacant hallways and public bathrooms...
controlled by a syringe of empty hope.
His muscles ached, his stomach pained.

Shivering and looking over Belmont Harbor
he realized the price had been too high.
He cried watching butterflies
as he faded away to a hopefully peaceful place.
Neil Young said it true,
"Every junkie's like a setting sun."

INDIAN SUMMER

Lazy clouds above,
flocking birds slice the sky.
They point south.
Young lovers hold each other close.

Ricing is done, the air is crisp.
Maples kaleidoscope red, yellow and gold.
Deer herds rest, move silently
and await the frenzied rut.
Partridges drum the fall air
and otters play on river's edge.
A turtle straddles a log
paying homage to the fading sun.
Cattails dance with wind.
Senses keen like a sharp knife blade,
Coyote is laughing, his fur is thick.

A moose stands in water, eating.
The rut is soon to come.
His love-call echoes the bush.
Smokehouse is busy.
Quiet trappers oil their traps.
A bush man splits wood for winter's blast.
Grandmother collects herbs for teas.
Crow celebrates with a serenade
that bounces through the bush.

Endings and beginnings.
It's Indian summer. *Aho! Aho!*

DANCIN' GIRL

With silent step rippling over soft moss,
I come to you,
clutching need to my chest.
Dancing in your private world
where I can only watch,
your small feet dance rapidly and soft.
A song trembles to silence
on your sweetened lips.
You await my touch.
The quick beating of your heart
whispers a song of invitation
that only my Ojibwa ears can hear.
You perfume your delicate body
with sweetness of cedar boughs.
You open your blanket silently
like the day's morning mist.
The trail of your hand
glows red like the glow of dawn
as you caress my shoulders, my chest.
Red mists of the setting sun
herald the ending of our perfect day.

Dancin' girl. Dancin' girl.

PROFESSOR MIKE BROWN

"Mike Brown's neighborhood
for those with no neighborhood":
a bustling, babble of vendors and deals,
a glaring, neon-illuminated
spectacle of racial paranoia,
a dirty place with bigotry graffiti
on cold damp concrete.
Young boys look for role models,
but find dope-man's greedy hand
to choke away hope and humanity.

Uptown, young girls captivated
by sweet logic are turned to whores.
I've heard the haunting words,
a melodic claim that "a money-makin'
whore deserves respect."
Sick, illogical minds
play sick games with young girls.

And yet! And yet!
You're the best of humanity,
you're the worst of humanity,
a carnival reflecting the human state.

WII-JII-WAA-GOON

Anishinaabe-kwe on your blanket,
I snuggle close
to the comfort of your bosom
listening to the beating
of your native American heart.
Wii-jii-waa-goon, it whispers, *wii-jii-waa-goon.*
Anishinaabe-kwe, on your blanket
I experience your womanhood.
Thrusts of desire are like ancient rhythms.
Wii-jii-waa-goon, our song, *wii-jii-waa-goon.*

VULGAR BULLETIN

Windy night-rain batters my face.
I was kissed passionately by a junkie whore
refusing to understand
that I was not the cure she craved.
Like a split decision she ran
her wretched tongue inside my mouth.
The taste of her was foul
with deceit and some sense of evil.

Her need was like a shy orphan
with enormous powers of resolution.
Her soul was an "ill-spirit" clinging to hope
that advanced, retreated
then kneeled humble on swollen knees
to pray for a martyr's funeral.

Lost on a path of broken promises
and panting furiously in fear,
she crawls on her belly
through vomit that serves as a laurel.
"Survive," she cries. "Survive."

WORDS OF LOVE

Don't think ourselves martyred souls, you and I.
We mingle our passion,
our laughter, our dreams
and we read each other's poetry.
As we lie naked side by side,
my eyes caress contours
of your pretty face and sweet body.

Your passing smile haunts
the hollow empty spot
and fills my being
with a boyish ardor
typical of my country style.

"And so, my dear lady poet,"
I whisper words of love.
"You've become the imaginary
queen of my Sunday mornings."

ALWAYS TOOK HIS TO GO

Walking in shoes of a man
damaged by the winds of life,
he installed security gates
on his emotions.
A solitary man, his intimate friends
are a three-legged alley cat
and a parrot with a broken beak.
He kept his back against walls.

Nasty Nellie whispers, "Ride a wild horse,
dare to be naughty in the night."
Lace, bared flesh and black silk,
moans of pleasure, warm moments,
with cocaine burning every breath,
she dreamed of the fast lane,
with a body built for business,
and head full of sin.

Front page news was that she'd
turn him inside out.
Hustlers were taking bets
but foolishly they forgot
he always took his to go.

In the end, she rolled dead
into the rivers of depravation,
lured by a Southside pimp
bragging of twenty whores
and an orchid-colored Cadillac.
The solitary man said nothing.
His world vision stored on ice,
not forced to confess true feelings,
he always took his to go.

SPECIAL RIGHTS

Special rights? You ask. I ask.
Treaty rights agreed to by your grandfathers
on their solemn oath.
As payment a cultures been taken
bite by greedy bite.
The pride and self respect were payment
and our land, too.

We remember Sand Creek,
Great Swamp and Wounded Knee.
We remember too
the Dawson Trail
and the heart-wrenching image
of granite hills raped of cover,
clear-cut by greed.
The stench of your profit
has poisoned the water, killed the ferns
and assassinated the moss
that so many Indians walked upon
with a gentle and loving step.

All a part of your demands.

Special rights? You ask. I ask.
Paid for with lives:
King Philip, Tecumseh, Black Hawk,
and my little brother in Viet Nam,
promises made in 389 treaties yet unfilled.
You think the memories have been killed?
No reason for those so-called
special rights that you scream in protest about?
Special rights? You ask. I ask.
Remember those were guaranteed
and they were paid for in advance.

THIS ROOM

Smoking too many cigarettes.
Rounded windows with plants.
A picture shows a guy passed out.
"As Bill Sees It" in red
letters higher than my head.
"Sobriety and Beyond."

The long table knows truth of a thousand lies.
I stand up and leave this room.
A week later, back again in this room.
My head hurts from the night before.
I listen to snatches of conversation:
Confessions, advice , confessions, more advice
from clean-cut voices, strong with sobriety.
Others shake with fear and pain
and shame and blame
that they pile on themselves.
Speaking quiet words of remorse,
I sit slumped, peering with reddened eyes.

Regular supermarket women come in,
once flashy, slinky things like you drink with.
The picture says "Don't do it. Stay strong."
I vow that I will tuck this day away
without whiskey to ease pain and fear.
The radio sings an old dusty tune
"Chances Are Your Chances Are Mighty Good."
I decide to take a chance,
stick around . . . in this room.

RAINY DAY, CHICAGO

A rainy day in Chicago
sends me to Mac Donald's looking
at crowds of splashing feet.
Drinking coffee, smoking cigarettes.
Feeling like I'll meet someone,
a curious individual with
curious eyes and smile
uttering those hometown expressions
bringing me to life.
Searching almost frantically
for small snatches of conversations
like a junkie without dope,
thunder without lightening
I'm sitting in Mac Donald's looking out.

ANOTHER RAINY DAY

Walking down Wabash Avenue wondering
if anyone knows that I just came from
lecturing students at University of Chicago
talking about nothing
to students wanting nothing
but to memorize a fact or two
about a topic which they may never
discuss again in their whole lives.
I feel like a wire stretched taut
against my mind
squeezing away any ideas
that might germinate into a poem
I can read some day in the future.

WARRIOR'S WAR

Oh, stay away from me, would ya?
Still that hunger for romantic concepts.
You've sold your Indian soul . . .
it shows on your breath.
Your politics jump from your eyes.
Everyday figures of expression
become passionate exclamations
heard on airwaves.
The vision has been drowned,
sucked into a whirlpool of anemic lies.
Walls built, moats dug, these cannot hide
you from your own truth.

Make quiet your scream,
for richness in my Mother's flesh.
You dig deep.
Her scars are sore,
painful to cast eyes upon.
You've sold your soul.
What could have been
had our nations joined as one?
What beguiling lies did they tell you,
puppet government serving my enemy?

A POEM FOR TOM DA POET

on the occasion of his death

A gentle man, he was excited,
at times, about life.
Some girls don't like boys like him
but he'd only smile and say
"Ah, but some girls do."
Oh, I suppose, he'll be compared
with some kind of Bukowski
but I think the dude was
some kinda Indian.
He had a good spirit
and yet he was a scoundrel
in the way that we all are.

You couldn't meet him and then
walk away unaffected to forget.
He grasped life and swallowed
it up like it was a shot
of good sippin' whiskey
aged to perfection.
He was the kinda man
could extract luxury smokin'
a leftover cigarette butt
or pure pleasure from some woman's bed
knowing full well that he'd
walk away in the morning.
He was a scoundrel
in the way that we all are.

You couldn't meet him
and then walk away to forget,
nah, not him.
He'd do something,
maybe make a joke at you,

about you, for you,
but you'd remember him.
Schemes and dreams were his, all right.
Hell, he had more plots than
the BIA does treaties
they never intend to keep.
I knew I could trust what he told me.
Our deals were the kind you don't find
written on paper.
His word was always good enough,
an honorable exchange
that assured our survival
when survival was hard to find.
I'll always remember him like that.

If you ever heard him poetin'
then I know you'd never forget
the way he could light up the night.
His excitement was contagious.
His images grasped you by
your emotions and they never let you go.
He was an altruistic man when it came
to talking about hunger
because he knew it like we know
the sharp sting of northern winds
on a January night.
He understood the words of my poem
"Beggin' Change Robs Your Soul"
better than any man I ever knew.
But Lord, his poetry was always truthful
and poignant words that
you somehow knew bounced
from the walls of his heart.

It won't be soon
he'll be forgotten.

His spirit will dance
in our midst. We'll say
poetry about him.
We'll remember his smile.
We will recall his outrageous schemes.
Let us enjoy those things
about him that made each
of us love him.
Let's remember how he could
always tickle our emotions
in his special way.

SHRINKS AND *INDIOS*

He asked me
"Do you pull your vire?"

I fell off my chair.
Wrong answer and where am I going?
I didn't want to answer.
I was scared.
Wrong answer and I'm heading
to where they lock up
the criminally insane
      biting bars,
        struggling against the cuffs,
        wrapped in wet sheets
        in hot tubs of ice.

Yeah, shrinks and *Indios*.

FOOT SOLDIERS

We are the foot soldiers,
the clear-eyed assessors of our times.
Don't try to lecture me about
pride in being Indian.
You wrongly think that's
been drummed away,
chipped away,
stolen and deadened
by a dominant society
that belittles our history,
beliefs and culture.
It's a vicious cycle
but don't worry friend,
my pride is intact.

Don't talk to me
about grand political objectives
or past atrocities.
I've lived the history
for one too many battles.
My elders were victims,
are victims.
now I sing to my babies
that sovereignty is taken,
assumed and not given
by a Brooks Brother's suit.

We are the foot-soldiers...
the clear-eyed assessors
of our times.
I don't want to focus
on the broken promises
or that cop who
wants to bust my head.

47

Those are realities
that I live with everyday.

I would rather see the image
of my brothers and sisters
standing proud, side by side.
Their laughter and smiling faces
illustrate the real character
of my people.
Not those school book pictures
of scowling hate-ridden skins.
It's those smiles that evoke admiration
of each other's imagination
and daring and courage.
It's the laughter that echoes
the drama, sacrifice, hope
and our small triumphs.

We are the foot soldiers,
The clear-eyed assessors of our times.

THIRD SHIFT
Dedicated to my respected elder Carlos Cortez

Ya know, old man,
you aged inspiration who never complains,
I've watched you over the years.

I been amazed at the way
your spirit rises and makes us all
better poets and thinkers.

Your "Third Shift" poem
I know from deep inside me
because I been there,
sleepy-eyed and hung over
and cussing the bosses
with every thought I could think.

Those grave-yard shifts rob everyone
of vitality but in the process
we're given back a sense of determination.

NOT ON THE GUEST LIST
For Dennis Banks of AIM

Oh, but could we partake
of the democratic process
our ancestors gifted to them.
Someone slammed the door
on our ghetto world.
We're not on the guest list,
and resolution 204
sits hidden away like a dirty secret
hidden away deeper even than
the "license for sale" scam.
Now their arrogance
has been slung around our lives.
Now we're jumping through hoops
hoping for a measure of dignity.

We're fighting in a silent class war.
With a twist of the head they glance at us
then look away like we're unlisted numbers.
Chief Illinowick is the governor's hero.
"It's an honorable thing.
It's an honorable thing!!"
says the dishonorable bastard.
204! 204! 204! Don't lose sight of 204.
The hocus pocus is straight-armed to the side.

Is history about to be repeated?
Is Annie Oakley there
on the 9th floor at Clark and Randolph?
Who is that woman trying
to act like an Indian agent
with a loaf of bread,
a brick of commodity cheese,
a broken old concept of a treaty,

and a request for a powwow?
She comes off like a Prozac queen.

We came looking for solutions
with suggestions and good will we came.
Is it an annoyance when we ask for respect?
And now you are talking at us like
we are your personal Tonto's
in Hollywood buckskin. Slow down, Kemosabe!
It's dignity we came to talk about.
You were going to fulfill
House Resolution 204. That's the issue.
Not a powwow at State and Lake.

We are those sovereign savages
who won't buy your hype—
no seamless assimilation.
And NO GREAT WHITE FATHER.
No step-and-fetch can replace mutual respect.
Looking around seeing
the brown, black and white faces
of other uninvited guests,
we see a look of recognition.
A silent message is passed with a nod or smile.
A closed fist to the heart
and our mutual experience is there,
bared and visible and a threat.
We all know something has got to change
Let us make it be the removal of distrust
based on the color of our skin.
We're not on the guest list not any of us.

Oh but could we partake of the democratic process
that our ancestors gifted to them.

TOO MANY COWBOY MOVIES
Dedicated to a man of the elitist theater

So you're sitting behind
your big oak desk,
like some kind of theater guru.
Your shirt collar chokes you
and your air conditioner is noisy.
Twenty years you've sat there
and looked out over the ghettos
and contemplated bringing a gift.

Twenty years you sat
and dictated in your college world
where the squeaky-clean come
to make dreams at high prices.
You knew in your heart
that they came because
their mommas paid the way
but in your heart you knew
there was another world
that couldn't pay to hear your words.
You knew, but you never came
to feel the warmth of the torch
the young and deprived were carrying.

You sat...you sat...you sat.
protected from those urchin dreamers
who would dare to challenge,
to question your validity.

Too many cowboy movies.

CAMPSITE 1996

Trees and wind harmonize
in a summer night's song.
A chill rides soft winds,
a small fire snaps,
sparks jump into the air.
The day's end pulsates into night,
over the glassy surface of the silent lake.
A kingfisher sails to his home.

I'm gifted a brief slice of eternity.
A valley of vagueness unfolds.
I can only peer into it
and so I listen
hoping for revelation,
or is it verification
of what my elders told me?

STRANGE MOMENTS

1.

He stood viewing the world
in wild turbulent dimensions
and painted nudes on old Chicago bricks,
those ones made by Bohunks
with clay dug from the riverside
where Potawatomi Indians danced
in times of plenty.
He set up a series of mirrors
and invited selected souls
to contemplate life
on the end of a stick
like those popsicles
we had when we were kids.

2.

He stood viewing the dead waters.
The bones of dead babies
began to cry loud, wailing chants.
Small boys from a
government Indian school
ran through cedar trees
looking for their hair
and the familiar, comforting,
sound of their language.
They captured the boys in New Mexico
and turned them into machinists
at the Schwinn Bike Company
and gave them Navajo girls
trained as nurses.

3.

Chicago had a pizza panic
and mushrooms sailed free form

through contaminated air.
Six hookers gathered on North Avenue
snapping bubble gum and thighs
where Indians used to dance.
Some ghetto Indians set up a sweat lodge
next to the railroad tracks
on the west side
and sweated for nine nights
for peace and the chance
to touch an executive
from the Standard Oil Company.

4.

Shaman bears rolled in
from the Rocky Mountains
like an early morning mist.
They sat at the dead water's edge
dreaming about a dancer
in a blue overcoat
with a thousand of Vizenor's
mind-monkeys embroidered
on a velvet collar.
Militant Indians marched
through South Dakota
with a dozen bitch canines in heat,
a gift to the police dogs
and the National Guards.
FBI Agents got nervous
and asked a musician
with arthritic fingers
and crippled soul
to play a jazzy tune.
He sang about a revolution
and being angry.
Those who sang with him
float bloated in the dead waters.

Dream_Warrior '95

He watched his shadow
doing battle with shards
of broken glass and urban decay.
He cried out in fear
when his shadow faded
at the corner
of California and Foster
where a blue and yellow
Port-A-Potty sat stinking
in the summer sun.
Morning came and he boarded
a flight to Jackson, Mississippi.
Dream warrior eats
a baloney sandwich wrapped in foil
and rides the #92 bus to work.
Stands behind a roaring
Le Blonde engine lathe,
singing Indian songs
about dead memories.

HONOR WINGED BROTHERS

Anishinaabe hunters sip coffee,
talking in whispered tones.

> Chemical cast-asides of humanity
> assassinate the Loon's senses.
> He peers with red eyes
> in dirty waters.
>
> Under a humid sky,
> he swims, he dives, and he calls
> to listening ears:
> "Must nature mirror humanity's
> tendency to self-destruct?"
>
> Tired, hungry and weakened,
> Loon opens his mouth to sing.
> No song comes forth.
> The jubilation's been muted.
> He spreads majestic wings,
> but flight eludes him.
> With red eyes he pleads,
> but the world's ears are deaf.

Anishinaabe hunters sip coffee.
They say with quiet tones
"He's a special messenger
who asks us to renew spiritual ties
to all our brothers and sisters
and to Mother Earth."

With voices robed in respect,
Anishinaabe hunters sip coffee and talk.
"He's that sacred messenger,
whose songs echo time, whose red eyes mirror

a confusing succession of trespasses
that cannot be forgiven.
"If we let this happen,"
the hunters whisper,
"mankind will lose again."
The Loon's song in the night
is a spiritual reminder.

Heed it well.
Honor our winged brothers.

CHILI CORN

She took it until her broken bones
and broken heart
ached like an old woman,
her dream of Prince Charming shattered.

The bruises reminded her
that man had created God in his image.
She took it—the hitting, the choking.
The degrading lasted for oh so long
she forgot how to smile
from deep inside where smiles are hidden.

Who holds hostage
those dreams she dared to dream?
What nature of assassin
choked to near blindness
those visions of hers
and altered them so she
could not recognize them?
The woman, *Anishinaabe-kwe*,
the sister's warrior spirit,
pushes her forward.

I'm in recovery, she thinks, from the war.
Kicked and choked and socked,
she tries to comprehend
the nature of her enemy.
Her lover?
Her tormented tormentor?
No answers make sense
and so she walks away
with the glint of purpose
in her Indian eye,
and the whisper of hope in her ear.

BORDERS

Lying on soft cooling moss
surrounded by a galaxy of ferns
and looking up at clouds,
borders were incomprehensible.
"Clouds hold only moisture," the scientists say.
But those clouds were sacred messengers,
and we were toddlers,
holding tightly a favorite blanket.
Remember when borders didn't exist?

Annabelle Rose, my baby girl,
plays contentedly on the kitchen floor.
Rays of sunlight dance with her attention span.
She picks them up, puts the sunrays away
saving them for another moment.
The beauty of her innocence
is like waking up to find
life worth the anticipation.
I realize for her
borders are incomprehensible.

Looking out my window,
searching for a sign
I reach deep down inside me
pulling up small pieces of Indian.
I know I can do as I must
to assure the sunlight is hers.
Together we cross borders.
Holding her in my arms protectively
borders are unthinkable.
The world is hers.
Remember when borders were
Incomprehensible?

ACCESSING IMAGINED HISTORY
Making It a Good Fight

I imagined community,
a history of gun-slinging heroes.
The Rambo's of earlier years
amount to invented Nationalism
and form the basis of America's male identity.
Rooted in lies and wishful thinking,
those out-on-the range fabrications
must leave you shivering
and your feet hurt
when you walk on the land.
Everywhere you step, the slivers
of that big lie stick
in your psyche and you stumble.

After the dust settled
from the cattle drives, forced marches
and development projects
you looked for the likes of me
to become reflections of you
and swallow the lies, but we didn't,
couldn't, and the images
always made us regurgitate.
There was no seamless assimilation
that was hoped for.
Even now we sometimes slip into a place
where our humanity is cast aside
and the cowboy mentality
comes into play.

Please don't make the Simpleton's error
of looking at us with nostalgic eyes.
We're here with you.

Don't accept those Hollywood perceptions
as gospel truth.
Hey, listen up pal,
we're not vanishing like early morning mist.
Humanity doesn't ever dissipate.

This whole "Amerika" story
is a tale about real estate.
The emotional center of it all
is about real estate.
The whole intersection of our races
is about real estate,
land coveted.
It was a cultural imperative
that illustrated its vanity
in biblical terms
like manifest destiny, but
when stripped bare it is nothing more
than imperialist positioning like
those leftists like to scream about.
colonialism at work.

Deceptive practice wrapped neatly
in that imagined community,
that invented nationalism
reinforced by Hollywood movies.
If we can see that
then we cannot be victims
stripped of our humanity.

TO RICHARD'S GUEST

Wearing your sickness
like beaded earrings,
you hiss demands
in a frustrated voice.
Richard and I stand
on the edge of Turtle Island
where the beach looks like
it was painted by an artist
with a bleak world view,
or maybe it's your voice.

We discuss Estera
in quiet tones.
The docile color
of his predicament
splashes his way
into the moment's mood
which sinks like our heels
into the beach's perpetual movement.

I wish she would dream
herself out of the darkened corners
of her self pity.
Players in the real world
dance when the rain
washes the slate clean.

I know you know
that I see your sick hustle.
You wouldn't last a minute
on the streets of Chicago.
Some fast-talking dude
from any part of town
would have you out there
learning the world owes you nothing.

WALDEN'S POND

Where pools of sunlight
linger on Walden's Pond
I wonder where the sound
of you went.
I realize I have to leave
this realm and enter
the dream world,
but they're clearing the pond
at eight thirty, I'm told.
Anyway, is dreaming really
a way into a memory?
Does memory dance a two-step
through the red nation's consciousness?

I'm this Indian guy
dancing through the jails,
and the bars with poems
in my hand and I wonder
if the dream will ever end.
My words are like the rattlesnake
that you could never tame.
The differences that you see
in my eyes, hair, and skin
violate your need for sameness.
The story of my survival
is riddled with bullet holes,
knife wounds, and ruptured emotions.
This balancing act I perform
in jails or saloons
makes me hard to look at,
rough to hear, but when I'm done,
I hope we will be a more complete
community of communicators.

UNFORGIVEN

I can't remember how I escaped
the lurching agony of days past,
before I realized there
are no remedies
to magically cure my wrongs.
No holy water sprinkled on my sin.
Mine was a black-colored motivation
imprisoned between
what feels good
and what is regarded by
scowling preachers as immoral.

She lies there asleep
in a cheap motel.
Her reddened hair cascades
down her small back.
My hand trails
the luscious curve
of her hip the roundness
of her behind.
The night wind stirs
the curtain and caresses
our nakedness.
She stirs slightly.
I count the small breaths
she takes before
she settles back to her sleep.
I realize that there is
no need for forgiveness
and kiss her gently
before I get up to leave.

YA CAN'T NEVER GO BACK

Sat in an LA alley listening
to a broken-hearted Chippewa boy
play road-blues songs,
strumming a beat up guitar
he called "my gitfiddle."
It was twenty-five years ago
and the storm in his songs
still make me feel good echoes.
We gave from the soul
in that alley in LA.
What goes around comes around,
the circle encased
in unforgiving concrete, steel and glass.

The brand new strings on his ax
testified to the man's soul.
Mellow sounds touched
me deep where only the sacred visit.
Those high *'Shinob* notes
and minor chords became
wind caressing birch leaves
in the intimate way
true relatives do.

The kiss of the southern sun
was a shared experience
and my words and his music
danced past the rats, grime and crime.
Someone slid in a 49er.
Our hearts beat to a drum,
the circle encased
in unforgiving concrete, steel and glass.

RAMBO TO FLAMBEAU

Spirit of northern lakes
churned in anger
as PARR people, wrapped in flags
and singing songs of hate,
entered a new day of racism
at Wisconsin landing sites.

A lynch mob of Amerikans—
high-strung in Kodiak boots,
plaid shirts, and shotguns—
ride dangerous and deadly
in pickup trucks.
Souls of hate glisten like silver gun racks
in war wagons with bumper stickers that say
"Save a deer, shoot an Indian."

Blood stains chrome.
Dancing flames glare
in Wisconsin's nights.
The metaphysics of racism
is based on the real estate aspirations
of the powers that are.
Who, though, made one race the classifiers?
Who decides how to categorize us
or to tuck comfortably away
those images that no longer sell?
Who so arrogantly believes
they can divide us all like that.
Our sons and daughters of every generation
seek to love and yet arguments float about
and we're divided
into national spheres of colonization.

"Rambo to Flambeau!" they shout

with weapons held at "Ready, aim, fire!"
The issue is hardly about walleyes.
Always scared
all the way to the bone
and even to the marrow
the hate-filled messages sound menacing.
Tension squeezes in alongside the fear
and ignorance is pure
and sung in a raspy voice
that grates on the mean souls.

Bleeding flames of hate
from sky-blue eyes,
they scream in protest against treaties
they don't understand,
victims of a deleted history
that's been stripped of truth.

They scream in the night
"Rambo to Flambeau! Rambo to Flambeau!"

Everyone is a product of environments.
Wrong perceptions dance,
and those old Indian images,
pressed into the hereditary memory,
jump out at us in full color,
through words like "savage,"
"murder," "revenge" and "heathens."
Anthropological misconceptions.

With spatulas of deception
they stir fires of distrust.
Brewing a formula of racial
and economic insecurity,
they spread fear and hate rumors
based on outright lies

that flutter about in northern winds
like fallen leaves
that stick to hunter's boots on rainy days.
Collected experience through words
like "savage, "murder," "revenge," "heathens."

"Rambo to Flambeau! Rambo to Flambeau!"
they scream and wave flags.
with weapons held at "Ready, aim, fire!"
The issue is hardly about walleyes
The intent anything but honorable.

Flags waving, they scream
"Rambo to Flambeau! Rambo to Flambeau!

MUSIC OF LIFE

Standing, listening atop a high hill
in a birch grove,
I'm feeling and listening to night sounds.
Creamy and full, the moon's image
dances on the shadowy lake,
depicting a feather-like final rendezvous.

Day wanes in silent retreat
to rest, to sleep, to recharge.
Moon beams glow in night sky.
Silence slides from the moon,
a mirrored ballerina of dark hues dancing.

I listen to the sounds,
looking around at this place
where in boyhood times
I prepared for the trip ahead.
I prepare, I prepare as I say good-bye.

The moment is drenched
in a shawl of near regret.
A child laughs.
Somewhere I hear a screech
and I realize I must dance
forward to face the music.
I am a dancer destined
to dance to life's music.

MEMORIES

Sitting in a gin mill thinking 'bout you,
a witchy woman
like those rock-and-roll boys sing about.
Oh, you were something special
passing through my world like a lightning bolt,
shattering my reality into small bits of regret.
Your song lulled me to sleep.
Your passionate embrace
woke every fiber of my being.

I wonder what I'd do if you
walked through that door?
Probably play cool, hoping you'd jump
at my smile and wit
but everything is so benign in daydreams.
I was caught up in your fast flowing river
of deceit and swimming against the current...
wishing hands of time could be reversed,
but wait a minute here, I don't want these hostile
thoughts.

Hell I liked the adventure...
the quickness of breath that your caress initiated.
Oh still in these quiet moment I recall your touch
those quiet sighs and urgent whisperings...
those memories come back to haunt me
like old rock-and-roll songs.
The softness of your love-making smile.
I recall the brown smoothness of your skin...
the sweat trickling between your Indian breasts
urging me to fill your needs.
Like other treasured boyhood memories
they're tucked away in pockets of my mind.

Sweet memories scented
with strawberry perfume and excitement.
They're all there for me when I want them
like this very moment sitting in this bar.

CRANDON IS A *WINDIGO*

The Holyman is chanting
The politician is ranting
The *Windigo* is panting

"Throw away that treaty!
Antique that piece of paper!
Put it in a museum!"

In a land where jack pine centurions
stand guard,
the Crandon Mining Company
struts through
with mineral detector flashing :
like lights in an old Flash Gordon movie.

Beware!
Beware you Wisconsinites!
You, Indian boy, listen up!
A deadly monster stalks
what your fathers went to war about.

With powerful arguments and powerful friends and
politicians in his pocket
Willie Crandon shuts his ear
to your public statements.
He throws employment opportunities,
like your Grandfather's cast seeds
into the fertile Wisconsin soil.

Your mother's mother dreamed
of a farm to feed the nation
that rode on the farm-hand's back.
Crandon dreams of dollars
and plays wolf in a sheep's skin.

He doesn't care about your dream
of two-and-a-half children
at play in the pristine playground
Mother Earth so conveniently provided.
Your robust smiles and happy hearty "ayes"
will turn to screams of despair
if Crandon has his way.
"Who?" You'll cry.
Whose dreams so badly wound our souls
and leave Mother Earth in pain?

Willie Crandon is a *Windigo*!
the real "money-money" junkie
that my brown-faced sister sings about.
Did you hear the words?
Buffy knew the facts.
She was right on track.
Money's just like crack.
Willie Crandon is a *Windigo*!

Years ago
in the *wigwams* of northern Indians
they talked quiet, cautious words
about the *Windigo*'s damage.
He creates big-time problems,
reddens the sky,
and steals your mind.
He creates famine in the land of plenty.
He'll take gentle dreams and create a nightmare.
Yeah! Willie Crandon is a *Windigo*,
a master of deception
a gangster of thought.

It's a mean game the *Windigo* plays.
He turns those fears to a craze
and gets his kicks on dark and cloudy days.

Yeah! Willie Crandon is a *Windigo!*
He keeps misery in his pocket.
He mixes it with dirty old dollars.
Remember,
Willie Crandon is a *Windigo.*
He's talking to your senator!

AFTERWARDS

E. Donald Two-Rivers (1945-2008), whose birth
name was Edmund D. Broeffle, grew up in the tra-
ditions of *Anishinaabeg* (Ojibwa people) on the Seine
River reserve in Ontario. This is the primary fact of
his literary writings. When he moved to Chicago, at
age sixteen, he lived in Chicago's Uptown neighbor-
hood as an urban Native person. Throughout his var-
ied career, which included prison and literary awards,
he was foremost an *Anishinaabe*. The *Chicago Tribune*
described the range of this poet's Chicago activities:

> Mr. Two-Rivers, who worked as a laborer for many
> years before becoming a journeyman machinist, par-
> ticipated in the symbolic occupation by Native Ameri-
> cans of the Belmont Harbor missile site in Chicago in
> 1971 and in the 1990s worked with the American In-
> dian Business Association and as an organizer with the
> American Indian Economic Development Association.

He drew upon this life experience for his poetry and
drama.

Critic Philip Heldrich writes: "The poems of Two-
Rivers have an urban edge. He writes streetwise po-
ems of protest and red pride" (*American Indian Culture
and Research Journal 2003*). Heldrich describes how
Two-Rivers' style is not contrived from metaphoric
language, but rather "cuts through a fog of false ide-
ologies in an attempt to discern truth by revealing its
opposite." This poet was a social critic, and he spoke
directly. Like *Diné* (Navajo) poet Luci Tapahonso, he
was a master of selecting images that suggest entire
stories. He could compress longer stories and political
views into bursts of lyric poetry. Like fellow Canadian
Neil Young, he found memorable phrases to penetrate
the minds of his listeners. Many of his poems are

built from parallel sentences, beginning with the same phrase, so the repeated sounds become unforgettable. These suggest the momentum of his performances.

I was fortunate to meet Eddie Two-Rivers in Chicago and to hear him read poetry when he was in his prime. He was one of the best performers I have seen—he had the ability to gauge his audience and attune to it, in the sense of David Antin's term "tuning"—to denote a performer's adjustment to the place and moment. Two-Rivers read for an academic audience at the Newberry Library, and later he told me he had shifted the reading to fit the group: he began with some political works, lightened the pace with calmer poems about Chicago (birdwatching along the lake shore), then shifted to serious works before ending with a dash of romance. From his experience as a playwright, he knew a performance arc well. The *Chicago Tribune* reported that he was "A regular and manic performer at the poetry slams at the Green Mill tavern in Uptown, 'He'd move up and down the aisles, back and forth, always moving,' and usually nicely dressed in a suit, writer and friend Mark LaRoque said. 'He would get loud.'" Everyone knew when Eddie was in a room.

Several years later, after he became ill, I saw him extemporaneously perform poems and monologues for a conference banquet, walking among the tables and charming everybody. He was charismatic, yes, but also substantive. Two-Rivers articulated the opposition between heartless bureaucracy and working-class people of all backgrounds. He foresaw corporate bankruptcy scandals like Enron and Wall Street bailouts in his poem "Crandon Is a *Windigo*," using this Ojibwa cannibal to embody greed. Heldrich notes his hard edges: "Two-Rivers' voice is directly in the tradition of protest authors or poetry of witness. He seeks to set the record straight, to confront oppression by acknowledging the pride of his roots."

Two-Rivers is a hero. He was *Anishinaabe*, or *"'Snob,"* during a time when that identity was especially difficult; he was Wolf Clan; he was son of a medicine woman; and he loved his family. He took the best parts of his experience and used them to transform his own life and to leave a body of literary works—poetry, plays, short stories, and journalism—to encourage others to stand up for justice,. He remembered his mother's advice in "Mom's Poem: Another Muskie Landed": "'Don't you ever be afraid to do what is right.'"

Denise Low, 2009

Anishinaabemowin   Ojibwe Language

Aho	An intertribal word that is said at the end of formal pronouncements. It is sometimes translated "Thanks" or "Amen."
Anishinaabe	Ojibwa. This word is from the Algonquin language family. _Anishinaabeg_ (plural) originally lived in Canada and the northern United States wherever birch trees grow.
Anishinaabe-kwe	Ojibwa woman
Dikinaagan	Cradle. Plural is _dikinaaganan._
49er	A song improvised for an informal gathering after a powwow, often with a romantic theme.
Ka-We-Goon-A-Bek	Approximately: First Snow, a woman's name
Kwe	A word ending denoting a woman. The noun is _ikwe._
Ma'iingan	Wolf
Miigwech	Thank you. Sometimes spelled "Megwech."
'Shinob	Slang for an _Anishinaabe_ person
Sapawe	Anglicized word for _zaasijiwan,_ running water. This is a small town in Ontario
Wabooz	Rabbit. _Plural is Waaboozoog_
Windigo or _Wiindigoo_	A giant winter monster who is a ravenous cannibal.

E. Donald Two-Rivers (1945-2008) is an original Native
writer with experiences both as a traditional person
(*Anishnaabe* or Ojibwa from northwestern Ontario)
and urban Indian. He moved to Chicago when he was a
teenager, where he worked and participated in arts and
civil rights movements. He led open-mic poetry readings
and performed his own verse. In the 1990s Two-Rivers
founded the Red Path Theater Company, for which he
acted, directed, and wrote plays. His honors include
the American Book Award from the Before Columbus
Foundation in 1999 for *Survivor's Medicine* and the Iron-
Eyes Cody Award for Peace, 1992. He lived in Green Bay,
Wisconsin, from 2002 until his death in 2008.

Plays

Briefcase Warriors (University of Oklahoma Press 2000)
    includes these plays: *Winter Summit or the Bang-Bang
    Incident; Forked Tongues; Chili Corn; Coyote Sits in
    Judgment; Shattered Dream;* and *Old Indian Trick , or
    An Old Urban Indian Story as Told by an Old Urban
    Indian Who May Have Lied*
Other plays are: *I Ain't Tonto, No Honors Today, Peeking Out
    Of Amerika's Museums, Pow-Wow Posse, Red Requiem
    - A Political Intrigue on City Streets,* Sunka Cheslie
    *(The Urban Pile) Survivors' Medicine, What's Buzzin'
    Cousin?,* and *Winter Summit.*

Poetry

A Dozen Cold Ones (chapbook from MARCH/Abrazo Press
    of Chicago, 1992)
Powwows, Fat Cats, and Other Indian Tales (Mammoth, 2003
    available at www.mammothpublications.com)

Short story collection

Survivors' Medicine (University of Oklahoma Press, 1998)

MAMMOTH PUBLICATIONS BOOKS

Barnes, Barry *We Sleep In a Burning House: Poems* $10
Day, Robert *We Should Have Come by Water: Poems* $15
Low, Denise & Tom Weso *Langston Hughes in Lawrence: Photos & Biography* $15 paper, $25 hardcover
Low, Denise, ed. *Ad Astra: Kansas Poetry Anthology* $12
Low, Denise *New & Selected Poems* (rpt., 2nd ed.) $15
Milk, Theresa *Haskell Institute: 19thCentury Stories* $20
Mirriam-Goldberg, Caryn *Landed: Poems* $10
Schultz, Elizabeth *White-Skin Deer: Hoopa Stories* $10
Two-Rivers, E. Donald *Fat Cats, Powwows, & Other Indian Tales: Poems* $12

Order Online:
www.mammothpublications.com (Pay Pal)

Mail Order, add $3:
Mammoth Publications
1916 Stratford Rd. Lawrence, KS 66044